GOD'S LITTLE bug GARDEN

Tune: Bingo "B-I-N-G-O"

Tiffany Monique Crosley

WestBow Press books may be ordered through booksellers or by contacting:

WestBow Press
A Division of Thomas Nelson & Zondervan
1663 Liberty Drive
Bloomington, IN 47403
www.westbowpress.com
844-714-3454

Because of the dynamic nature of the Internet, any web addresses or links contained in this book may have changed since publication and may no longer be valid. The views expressed in this work are solely those of the author and do not necessarily reflect the views of the publisher, and the publisher hereby disclaims any responsibility for them.

Any people depicted in stock imagery provided by Getty Images are models, and such images are being used for illustrative purposes only.
Certain stock imagery © Getty Images.

ISBN: 978-1-6642-1128-5 (sc)
ISBN: 978-1-6642-1132-2 (e)

Library of Congress Control Number: 2020921654

Print information available on the last page.

WestBow Press rev. date: 11/09/2020

WestBow
PRESS®
A DIVISION OF THOMAS NELSON
& ZONDERVAN

THIS
book
BELONGS TO

Tune: Bingo "B-I-N-G-O"

GOD'S LITTLE bug GARDEN

God made a little marching ant and placed it in his garden,
March, march little ant,
March, march little ant,
March, march little ant,
Marching through the garden,

God made a little butterfly and placed it in his garden,
Float, little butterfly,
Float, little butterfly,
Float, little butterfly,
Floating through the garden,

God made a little spider and placed it in his garden,
Climb, little spider,
Climb, little spider,
Climb, little spider,
Climbing through the garden,

God made a little bumble bee and placed it in his garden,
Buzz, little bumble bee,
Buzz, little bumble bee,
Buzz, little bumble bee,
Buzzing through the garden,

God made a little ladybug and placed it in his garden,
Crawl, little ladybug,
Crawl, little ladybug,
Crawl, little ladybug,
Crawling through the garden,

God made a little grasshopper and placed it in his garden,
Hop, little grasshopper,
Hop, little grasshopper,
Hop, little grasshopper,
Hopping through the garden,

God made every creeping thing
that creeps upon the earth,
B-U-G-S,
B-U-G-S,
B-U-G-S,
God placed them in his garden.

God made a little dragonfly and placed it in his garden,
Fly, little dragonfly,
Fly, little dragonfly,
Fly, little dragonfly,
Flying through the garden,

God made a little lightning bug
and placed it in his garden,
Blink, little lightning bug,
Blink, little lightning bug,
Blink, little lightning bug,
Blinking through the garden.

About the Author

Author Tiffany Monique Crosley currently resides in Eastern North Carolina with her family, where she is active in her local church, teaching children's Bible classes, teaching puppet ministry, and participating in community outreach projects. Tiffany received an Early Childhood Associate Degree from Carteret Community College and received her Bachelor of Science in Human Services with a concentration in Child & Family Welfare from Kaplan University. Tiffany has over 20 years of experience working in the fields of Early Childhood Education, Youth Recreation Programs, Child and Family Services.

Printed in the United States
By Bookmasters